Eyes Wide Shut
It Happened to ME

My Journey to Freedom

Deneshia Clemons

Copyright © 2022 Deneshia Clemons

Book Package and Publication
Leadership DevelopME, LLC: www.leadershipdevelopme.com
Book Cover Design: Aikhuele Einstein

All rights reserved. No part of this book may be used or reproduced by any means, graphic, electronic, or mechanical, including photocopying, recording, taping, or by any information storage retrieval system without the written permission of the publisher except in the case of brief quotations embodied in critical articles and reviews.

Books may be ordered through booksellers or by contacting:
Deneshia Clemons
Website: www.houseoflovinghands.org

Because of the dynamic nature of the Internet, any web addresses or links contained in this book may have changed since publication and may no longer be valid. The views expressed in this work are solely those of the author and do not necessarily reflect the views of the publisher, and the publisher hereby disclaims any responsibility for them.

Any people depicted in stock imagery provided by the Internet are being used for illustrative purposes only.

ISBN: 978-1-387-92108-9
Library of Congress Control Number: 2022912439

Printed in the United States of America

Scripture taken from The Holy Bible, KJV 1769 edition, public domain. Scripture taken from THE HOLY BIBLE, NEW INTERNATIONAL VERSION ®. Copyright© 1973, 1978, 1984, 2011 by Biblica, Inc.™. Used by permission of Zondervan

Scripture quotations are from] New Revised Standard Version Bible, copyright © 1989 National Council of the Churches of Christ in the United States of America. Used by permission.

All rights reserved

DEDICATION PAGE

I want to honor God, who is the foundation of my life.

To the ones that cause all four pieces of my heart to beat.....

De'Jhonea, JR, A'jheda, DeJohn

To my Grandmother (My Heart RIH), My Mother (Mother Dear), my Dad, my Bonus Mom (RIH), my Sissy's, my Family and Friends, thank you all for your love and support.

And to all the women that didn't make it, this book is dedicated to you.

Love, A Domestic Violence Survivor

TABLE OF CONTENTS

Prelude:	Who Me?..	1
Eye Opener 1:	The Glass Begins to Break................................	3
Eye Opener 2:	Tracing Abuse: A Little Family Problem....	17
Eye Opener 3:	Ring, Ring	23
Eye Opener 4:	Eyes Wide Shut	33
Eye Opener 5:	It's Not Just Black & White	41
Eye Opener 6:	My Darkest Night..	45
Eye Opener 7:	The Comeback..	53
Epilogue:	Wrapping It Up	61
References		63
Resources...		65
Author's BIO...		67

PRELUDE:

Who Me?

Here I am on my knees in the bushes in a park right around the corner from my house, where homeless men and women sleep. It's cold; I am cold, cowering down on the slimy wet dirt, where ants, worms, and just too many bugs underneath me. The thorns from the bushes are sticking and poking me in the face, arms, legs, and all over my body...oh my God! Because I left so quickly, all I had time to do was throw on some sweats. I didn't have time to put on a bra, panties, socks, or shoes. I was on my knees, peeking through the bushes. I watched as my car drove back and forth, looking for me. My heart was in my throat. It was beating so loud that I couldn't hear my own thoughts, and my stomach was so sick with fear that I vomited right where I was kneeling. But I couldn't move. I was sweating, praying, and holding my breath so my hiding place wouldn't be blown.

The whole time I am hiding in the bushes, thinking, *"How did I end up in this crazy mixed-up position?"* Like NAW SERIOUSLY, how did I end up on all fours like an afraid, wounded, beaten down dog?

Okay,
let me start from the beginning…

EYE OPENER 1:

The Glass Begins to Crack

Growing up, I always wanted the fairy-tale life, which included a house, a loving husband, children, cars, a career, and most of all, MONEY! However, that ain't what I got (sigh). In 1970, on August 5th, it was a warm and sunny day when I kissed the earth with my golden presence. I was born to Charles and Glenda Clemons. Sadly, they divorced when I was only four years old, so I didn't have that "American Family" that included a two-parent home.

Since my arrival into this world 50 years ago, nothing much has changed. Society established an image of what beauty looked like, and it didn't represent me. I looked around at the women in my own family, and they were caramel to fair-skinned and gorgeous. I didn't see how my dark skin could shine and be considered pretty, even in my lineage. I saw my baby pictures, and I was a cutie pie; however, as I began to grow older, I began to take on the falsehood that having dark skin was ugly. I was called so many nasty names by teachers, classmates, and even church kids. This was all within my community; then I had to gather up the courage and step out into a world that would treat me far worse than my community. I never understood the fear that many carried because I didn't look like them. Did somehow my color and presence diminish who and what they were in society? And the true answer is NOPE! Anyway, if you haven't guessed it, I grew up feeling like the black sheep of the family and society (LITERALLY!!!)

For years, it would just be me, my mom, and my baby sister. Around the age of 10 years old, we gained an older sister. Whew! Our lives have never been the same since her arrival. LOL. I'm sitting here thinking of the many stories we all have. The one that sticks out the most, is when our mom instructed me and my baby sister to clean up the house before leaving to go and spend time with our god-sister. Well, our oldest sister said, "You guys go ahead and get out of the house. Mom put me in charge, so you guys can leave. I will tell Mom that I said it was OK." BAE BAE as soon we got to our destination, we got a call from Mom asking why we left the house without cleaning it. All happy voiced, we said that we were told it was OK to leave. All we heard was, "IF Y'ALL DON'T GET Y'ALL TAILS BACK OVER HERE NOW!!!!!" Our stomachs were sick as we walked back home over hills and through the mountains to our death sentence. Once we got home, it was on and cracking.

As soon as we opened the door, we were snatched up, and we got the devil beat out of us. My baby sister was on the kitchen floor spinning around in circles while getting whooped, and I'm running around the dining room table practicing for a chance at the Olympic Track and Field Medal, trying not to get hit. As we felt like our lives were coming to an end, we looked over at our oldest sister only to see her with the phone pressed to her ear, pretending like she was talking on the phone with somebody with her body pressed so hard against the wall, that she almost disappeared. She had the old school 20-inch phone cord wrapped around her body like a dress, and I'm thinking, *"Hey, authority speaker, start speaking because we're dying over here."* My Gawd! We cry laughing every time we think about this incident, and believe it or not, we have so many more stories like this that have bonded us with love to this day.

As my family size grew from three to four, here came a fifth person. My mom married my stepfather, S**T; oops! I almost cussed (don't judge me, I love Jesus, but I cuss a little). Okay, back to the story. HELL, where do I start...? I was around 15 years old when my mom got married. In the beginning, our stepfather was good. He was trying to be our best friend, but there was something about him that I couldn't place my finger on. He didn't give out good vibes from the gate. However, we found out fairly quickly that he was a narcissist, a woman beater, and just a mean and evil man. He took a shine to my baby sister and tried to buy her love, which wasn't for sale. And then there was me; he treated me like a slave, and it seemed that my very existence annoyed him. There were so many incidents where he showed me that he despised me.

I remember one time when I was fixing a sandwich for lunch and accidentally got mustard in the mayonnaise jar. When he discovered the atrocity, he stretched his arms high above his head and threw the glass jar of mayo into the kitchen sink. Glass and mayonnaise went everywhere. The thick white slime-looking substance was everywhere and on everything. As I stood in amazement, I couldn't believe that this joker did all of this because there was a hint of mustard in the mayonnaise jar. I slowly turned my head and looked over at him. He literally was jumping up and down, yelling, "What the hell is wrong with you? You're messing up the mayonnaise for the rest of us." I was flabbergasted that this grown man was having a temper tantrum over something so trivial. He told me to clean it up once he finished his Broadway show. I sucked my teeth and rolled my eyes at him. I rolled my eyes so hard that I was surprised they didn't get stuck in the back of my face. Lest we not forget, that every time he had an episode, my mother was never around. It got to the point that I started being the release of his frustration. When he was home, my sister and I couldn't laugh or talk too loud. We couldn't have friends over, and he used food that we liked as pawns. He would literally put sodas in the garage on the shelf and then park his car in front of the shelves to make sure that we couldn't get to them, and when he was feeling generous, he would let us have a can of soda, once the fizz was gone, and the drink was flat. This joker used to hold us hostage at the dinner table by trying to make small talk, just a skinning and grinning as we rolled our eyes in disgust, giving only one-word answers. This was all for show. This was his way of showing my mother how much he cared for us—what a freaking joke!

I also recall when my sister and I asked for a candy bar from the box of chocolates that he had bought from his job, and as always, his answer was no. So, about three months had passed, and he came into our room, which was located in the downstairs part of the house, and he is cheesing like a Cheshire cat and handed each one of us a chocolate bar. Yes, the ones that we had asked for months prior. In excitement, we ripped open the candy bars, and as you can imagine, the once silky milk chocolate bars were now white chocolate bars with specks of sadness and depression. I believe he got great pleasure at being a narcissistic jerk.

Whenever my stepfather had a bad day, he would argue with my mom; however, he never laid a hand on her. Unfortunately, that wasn't my story. I don't remember the first time he thought he would slap me and get away with it. But I recall him on many occasions trying to pick a fight with me, and with my smart mouth and my loathing feelings towards him, it just added more fuel to the fire. Well, on this particular day, I was just sick of him, and I chose violence. Because he was once again hurling mean and nasty things at me, and I said something that he didn't like, and he then hauled off and slapped the dog piss fire out of me. I said, to myself, self? Did this n***a just hit me? I, in turn, socked the crap out of him, and the fighting began. Mind you, we weren't raised in a home where people physically fought one another, so this was new and a culture shock. So, to say the least, my attitude and mouth grew worse and nastier as each fight ensued. I didn't realize that my stepfather was setting the stage to make me look like the rebellious teenager from hell to my mother, so that when he finally got the courage to begin trying to creep into my room, he would be able to attack my character and make it seem like I was the problem.

I was always walking on eggshells around him because I didn't know what I would do or say that would tick him off. My only relief was when I would visit my dad and bonus mom every summer. My trips to Inglewood, Los Angeles, always brought butterflies of happiness and peace. God blessed me with a bonus mom that loved and treated me as her own. (May she rest in Heaven). Despite me enjoying being spoiled by my dad and bonus mom, I didn't know that behind the scenes, that whenever I would visit my dad, my stepfather would wreak havoc by arguing with my mom and my dad about me spending the summer with my dad. He felt that I needed to be home. Huh? Are you kidding me?

In (1986) the year I turned sweet sixteen, my world would be turned upside down. It was that time again for me to go and spend time with my dad and my bonus mom for the summer, and I was so excited. I started packing and preparing my mind for vacation, only to get a call that no child should ever receive from their father. As I think back, I remember the phone ringing and my mom saying, "*Necey, pick up the phone.*" I was giddy when I heard my dad's voice, only to have the air sucked out of me as he began to speak. He stated that he was tired of fighting with my stepfather regarding seeing me. He then stated that he was going to step back out of my life for the time being and to give him a call when I turned 18 if I wanted him to be a part of my life. Then the phone went dead. I was devastated. My thoughts were, *Why didn't my dad fight for me? Does he even love me?* However, this was exactly what my stepfather wanted because this was the same year that he would try to sneak into my room and make his moves. I fought him every single time. I still remember having to put chairs under the doorknobs and locking all the doors that led to me because he was on a mission.

This was the same year when I lost another piece of myself. My beautiful grandmother, whom I loved with all my heart, had been thriving and living with breast cancer. She had to have both of her breasts removed ten years prior, but it didn't change her feistiness and heart for people. She lived life to the fullest. She was an excellent Registered Nurse (RN) and a Missionary in the church. When I tell you, she was the epitome of the word beautiful, inside and out. This woman loved me. She loved my smile, my walk, my talk, and black chocolate skin, at a time when being light skin was glorified and to be of dark complexion was automatically considered ugly.

On October 16, 1986, I received the worst news possible. My grandmother, my heart, and my second mom died after cancer returned (ladies, please get your breast checked yearly). My heart ached because the woman that meant the world to me had left me to face the world alone. I was in a daze for days. I remember going to school and not remembering how I had even gotten there. I remember walking down the school hallways crying, and everywhere I looked was like waterfalls. I couldn't believe that she was gone. I also remember calling my step-grandfather asking to speak to my grandmother because I called her every single day, and him just sitting on the phone in silence, and that is when it really hit me that the love of my life was gone. I was lost………..

About a month later, I suffered from a horrible toothache and needed to go to the dentist. At 16 years old, I had a work permit where I worked for the government for four hours and went to school for four hours. I told one of my co-workers that my tooth was killing me so bad, and she gave me half of her bottle of Tylenol with Codeine pills for the pain. Eventually, I couldn't take the pain anymore and went to the dentist, only to find out that all four of my wisdom teeth had to be removed. WAIT!!!! WHAT??? LAWD, TAKE ME NOW! However, before my regular dentist appointment to get my wisdom teeth removed, one of the wisdom teeth had gotten infected and began infecting the others. So, I made an emergency appointment and got all my problem teeth removed. As usual, I was given medicine for the pain. Once, I was healed and no longer living my days in a psychedelic haze, I was able to go back to school and work.

One day, I was sitting at my desk at work, and suddenly, things that I had been going through in life hit me hard. It began to play like a movie in slow motion. My heart got sad, and I was sitting at work, falling into a depression. I felt alone, unloved, and ugly. I felt like no one would even care if I no longer existed. So, I went to the bathroom on my job and took all the medicine that my co-worker had given me and all of the medicine leftover from my dental procedure, which equated to over 20,000 mg of pills.

I remember looking into the bathroom mirror and hating what was looking back at me. I was moving like a robot as I walked back to my desk and reached over to turn off the computer. I cleaned up my desk, bid my co-workers farewell, and walked to the bus stop in a fog. Once the bus arrived, I stepped on the bus heading home because, in my mind, I was just going to go home and die, and I wouldn't have to live in this pain anymore. But God had a different plan for my life because, while I was sitting on the bus, my stomach began to get queasy, and I was fighting, trying to hold the pills down. But before I knew it, I lost the battle, and I started throwing up all over the place. I threw up so much that I was dry heaving by the time I hit my doorsteps. On that day, my stepfather actually asked if I was okay, I said, no and told him what had happened, and he rushed me to the emergency hospital. But, oh my friends, he had the nerve to be fussing the whole way because, in his words, he had better things to do besides sitting in an emergency room. Are you serious? I won't even repeat what I said. On a positive note, I made it to the hospital. The doctors tried pumping my stomach, but it was empty. They asked me what pills I had taken, and they were astonished that I was still alive; they, even stated, I should have OD'd. As I think about the events that led to me trying to take my life, my feelings were valid (remember, never devalue the way someone feels because you don't understand their pain).

I did feel alone, misunderstood, and that I was an insignificant part of the family structure. However, at the same time, I did have family and friends that loved me, and all I had to do was muster up the courage to say HELP ME! Speaking up and out is not always easy, so if you ever feel like the pain in your heart is too heavy and you're thinking about taking your life, reach out and make a call first. There are people waiting to talk to you. (National Suicide Hotline 988).

When I turned 18, I did reach out to my father so that he could once again be a part of my life. Unbeknownst to me, this put an unconscious stamp on my life's journey passport on how I would begin handling all types of relationships going forward. They say girls look for their fathers in the men they choose, but I believe girls look for the bond established with their fathers when it comes to choosing their mates. In life, I found myself being the one that made relationships work. If you were/are my friend, I found myself being the one who reached out to see and make sure my friends were okay. I found myself being the one that did the calling for birthdays and the one wishing everyone Happy New Year (once I stopped that vicious cycle, some friend connections did too). And if it was an intimate partner/husband, I found myself going above and beyond to make sure that we were both happy. As we all know, that is a bumpy road to disappointment, failure, and disaster. A relationship will never last with only one person doing all the work. To me, a successful marriage takes God being the foundation, love, support, open communication with understanding, and two mature people who genuinely want each other and are committed to working together.

My glass of life was not just cracked, but broken by this time. I was ready to leave my place of trauma, and I ended up looking for validation in all the wrong places. Thinking I had found love, I ended up getting pregnant at twenty-one. I wasn't married, and because I was an unwed, expectant mother in church, I needed advice on what to do. I went to the elders of the church for sound counsel. Unfortunately, the counseling that was given was from a place of church tradition and through their own life experiences, not through an open mind and spiritual discernment. I grew up in an era where if you got pregnant and wasn't married, you were told the only honorable thing to do was to get married. Now that I look back on these practices, what comes to my mind is SAYS WHO? HONORABLE WHERE?!!! Honestly, if I knew then what I know now, I would never have gotten married.

But, uh yep, I too walked in that tradition and followed the elder's advice, and got married. I didn't know then that I had jumped from a greased black skillet frying pan directly into hell's fire. I didn't realize that without true counsel and therapy from my past traumas, I was beginning my adult life pregnant, and in a trauma induced state. In other words, I was starting life with Post Traumatic Stress Disorder (PTSD).

Open YOUR Eyes

What are some of your PTSD triggers?

_____
_____
_____
_____
_____
_____
_____

What tools can you incorporate in your healing journey, that will allow you to navigate through your PTSD triggers?

_____
_____
_____
_____
_____
_____
_____
_____
_____

EYE OPENER 2:

Tracing Abuse: A Little Family Problem

According to *Medline Plus, National Library of Medicine* (2021). Deoxyribonucleic acid (DNA) is the molecule inside cells that contains the genetic information responsible for the development and function of an organism. DNA molecules allow this information to be passed from one generation to another.

As I think about my connection with my ex-husband, I dissected both sides of our bloodlines, wondering where this abuse and trauma stemmed from. My mind reels back to my family's many divorces, some hidden secrets, and also a story of my uncle, who was smart as hell but heavy on drugs. I remember the night he held me, my sister, and my mom hostage, when he was on one of his drug-induced episodes. I remember that night like it was yesterday. My mom had let him stay with us because he had no place to go. My auntie had kicked him out and left him because he would fight her like he was trying to win the Las Vegas Boxing Match against Holyfield. I remember us coming home to discover that my uncle had stolen and sold our TVs, my mailbox piggy bank, and anything that he could get his hands on to get him enough money to buy more drugs. My mom was beyond mortified when she came home to see all of our stuff gone. She proceeded to kick him out, and that's when everything went to hell.

He had my sister and me trapped in our room and my mom trapped in her room, which was separate from us as he ranted, yelled, and screamed that none of us were leaving out alive. I don't know what got into me, but I took a deep breath and darted out of our room to be with my mom. That is when he came charging out of the kitchen with an eight-inch butcher knife. He swung the knife over his head and tried to stab me at the top of my head. He only missed me by a few inches. I didn't look back. I could only hear and feel the wind from the swinging of the knife. At this time, my mom was trying to navigate how to get to her babies. I was nervous because I had left my baby sister alone. My mom, a strong, intelligent, and beautiful woman, became the momma bear and hopped on my uncle's back, and there they went tumbling down the stairs. My uncle fought and swung the knife as my mom used her bare hands to grab the blade to protect herself, my sister, and me. We were crying and screaming because we didn't know what was happening and if our mother would make it out alive. Fortunately, our neighbors heard the fight and called the police. The next thing we knew, there were bells ringing and loud knocks at the door. The police came, and we were saved by the bell (literally). My mom's hands and body were bloody, cut up and battered, but she was alive.

My mind tried to think of other abusive situations through my bloodline and couldn't think of another time until I spoke with my father and found out that my paternal grandfather used to beat and humiliate my beautiful grandmother (my dad's mom). Until this day, we still don't know how she died. One morning she was alive, and by nightfall, she was gone. It's speculated that my grandfather may have killed her. There are many questions surrounding her death and, at the same time, no questions at all. But once again, it's speculation and not a topic really talked about.

Now that I've talked about my bloodline, let's get into the bloodline of the man I once called husband. Whew! Where do I start? We were young and thought we were in love, and as I began spending time with him and his family, family secrets (we all have them) began to emerge. I overlooked these red flags because I was pregnant and was advised to do the right thing. So, I plowed forward and married into this family. During my marriage, I experienced my father-in-law trying to make passes at me, cornering me at family functions, and offering me money if I would be nice to him. It got to the point that I would stay in the living room in their home during family gatherings in order to feel safe. Eventually, I stopped going to gatherings altogether. I learned that this bloodline dealt with infidelity, abuse, incest, and molestation. What do you do when you've already said, I DO? I am now carrying my second child, and now I'm feeling trapped because I didn't want God (in my mind), to be mad at me if I got a divorce, which is a misconception of who God is. Unfortunately, I stayed.

Remember, when dating, you should factor in your DNA and your partner's DNA because when procreation begins, we are responsible for the outcome of what our DNA makes. Please do not ignore red flags, be careful and wise about who you're joining in holy matrimony.

Open YOUR Eyes

What pieces of your lineage make up your DNA pattern?

_____
_____
_____
_____
_____
_____
_____
_____

What parts of your DNA help you to navigate through stressful situations?

_____
_____
_____
_____
_____
_____
_____
_____

EYE OPENER 3:

Ring,

So many women came in and out of my marriage while I tried to be a good, honorable wife and mother, only for me to be hit, degraded, and humiliated. How could a man that says he loves a woman treat her less than gum located at the bottom of his shoe, making her feel like nothing more than a nuisance and headache?

I remember being eight months pregnant with my first child, and while relaxing in our new apartment, basking in the moments from when we said, I DO, then the phone rings, and there was a woman's voice on the other end asking where my husband is? So, I asked, "Who are you, and what do you want? She said, "Well, I met your husband, and he said that I could call." I stated, "Do you not have any shame calling a married man? Don't call back here again." She then continued to say, "Well, he said that I could call, so if he said

I can call, I'm going to call." The nerve. Needless to say, I said a few words that I know my guardian angel kept looking at God, like that's all you. So, I hung up the phone and checked my husband for disrespecting me. You would think that he would have been shamed and consoling. Nope! He then punched me and slammed me on my back. Remember, I was eight months pregnant. All the air was forced out of me as I laid on the floor, feeling like I was dying and praying that my baby was okay. As I laid on the floor, shocked, pissed, angry, humiliated, and in pain, he grabbed his key and left. Later I found out he went to see the mysterious girl caller.

Another incident happened two weeks before Christmas. I had gotten off early from work, located in the city of San Francisco. As I was walking up to my door, I heard voices. I placed my keys in the door and swung the door open as hard as I could, only to find my husband and a woman chilling on the couch. Did I mention I'm the only one that worked and took care of the family? This N***a was in my house entertaining women like this was the Red Roof Inn. As I began walking towards him, the joker had the nerve to say, "Necey, it's not what you think. This is my best friend's girlfriend, and she was waiting at our house until her boyfriend got off work." Sir, your best friend is married with children. Who the F**k are you talking about? I went ballistic. My anger was towards him because that's who was supposed to be committed to me, not her. Plus, she looked scared as hell. But I guess my hurt and anger didn't mean anything because he grabbed this unknown woman's hand. Literally...grabbed her hand and guided her out the door. He wasn't seen again until 2:00 am. Some respect, HUH! And yes, that was a fistfight out of this world. Yet, I stayed.

I recall another situation where I would bring my children to daycare in Daly City, work all day in San Francisco, and travel home to Oakland by Bart every day. I worked hard while he did nothing but screw, eat, sleep and screw some more. His only job was to pick me and the kids up with my car when I got off work. Well, this didn't happen as planned one day after a long day at work. I waited at the Bart Station in Oakland with two small kids for over an hour. It was cold, and my kids were tired and hungry. There were no benches to sit down on, and I didn't have money to catch the bus, so I started asking people for money on the streets so that my kids and I could get home. I felt like a bum; I felt low and angry. Needless to say, he never showed up to pick us up, and we had to catch the bus with the money people were generous enough to give me.

When he finally got home, he walked into the house like he was King Ding A Ling. He had the audacity to act like he didn't understand why I was so mad. All the while, I kept thinking, this joker was just with the next woman , while he had his kids and his wife begging like a dog on the streets. BAE BAE, you know that ended in an all-out brawl. He had the audacity to feel that the words coming out of my mouth made him feel like less of a man and that I was being disrespectful. Well, let me break this down so it can forever and consistently be broken. He had nothing; wasn't doing nothing, and was nothing. The only reason he was blessed was because I was his favor. The car he was driving was the car that I paid for in full, and every morsel of food that this n***a ate was at the hands of my hard work. I certainly didn't have a problem letting him know that he was a trifling broke A** B***H, which made him mad. HA! Who cares? Because he knew he wasn't taking care of his family, and the only time he felt like something was when he was making me feel like nothing.

Okay, Good Lawd, am I still talking about my phone ringing? Okay, this one happened when we had a small church, and one of the members, who was a faithful young lady with a child, had gotten into a bit of trouble. The kind of trouble that landed her in the county jail for the weekend. Because she trusted us, so, I thought, she called to see if we could come and pick her up from jail. She said that she didn't have any money for a bus or cab ride.

Well, my husband at the time went ahead to go pick her up. I couldn't ride with him due to having two sick kids at home that I was nursing back to health. Sadly, I would find out later that year that when he went to pick her up, they were flirting with one another. And when he pulled up to her house, he made a hard pass at her. Sadly, she was down with the get down. The only thing that stopped them from doing the jingle jangle dance was that she was on her period, and this joker had the nerve to say something that I had told him that worked for my body. Something we discussed as a married couple. I told him that if a woman takes a warm bath while on her period, it would slow the flow long enough to get her freak on. When she repeated what I knew only me and him discussed, my mouth hit the floor. He was taking a private conversation with his wife and using it to get into yet another woman's pants. I was beyond embarrassed. Did he have no shame? I guess his body didn't carry the "shame gene" because he never stopped.

Geesh, the phone was ringing again, and there was yet another woman's voice on the line. She asked me where my husband was, and I said, "Who are you, and what is your point of calling?" She replied, "I just wanted to know if your husband left the house yet because he was supposed to be on his way over here." Then she said, "Oh, never mind, he is ringing the doorbell now." Then she hung up the phone in my face. I was holding the phone like, WAIT! WHAT just happened? My stomach was sick, and my body was hot with anger. So, I called that number back over 20 times (ladies please never do this), trying to get her back on the line, but she wouldn't answer. However, she did call to let me know she was sending him back home about an hour later after she was finished with him. I said, "B****H, who the F**k you think you're talking to!!!!" This woman was able to describe what my husband had on down to his drawers. I kept thinking that this was unbelievable. This is what movies are made of, not my life.

So, my husband casually walked into the house like he was the pimp daddy of the year. I asked him, "Where have you been?" Of course, he lied, saying that he went to his best friend's house because he and his wife were having problems. He didn't know that his best friend, who he was helping with marriage problems, had called looking for him.

So, I asked him again, "Where were you?" He continued to lie, and I was tired of him at this point. I said, "OK. I hope you had a wonderful evening with your woman." After that, I just turned around, went to the bedroom, and went back to bed. Then all of sudden, out of nowhere, he jumped on my chest, pinning my arms to the bed with his knees. *I was like, what the hell is going on?* Then he took out his community penis and said, "SUCK IT." Was this n***a on drugs? I said, "Hell Nah! Have your b***h at that house you just left, suck it." He told me, "If you don't B***h, I am going to pee in your face."

I rolled my eyes and said, "Whatever nasty a**." Before I could get the whole word out, HE PEED ALL OVER MY FACE. Pee was dripping in my eyes, down my face and ears, onto the pillow where I laid. I was mortified, I couldn't believe what just happened. I got up, swinging and punching while the pee was stinging my eyes as it ran down my face into my mouth. What kind of marriage was this? Did God, and the elders of the church that I went to for advice, really want me to stay in this?

I got up the following day thinking that I would go to work because I couldn't stand being home or around him anymore. Mind you, I packed me and my kid's bags the night before. I was leaving for the umpteenth time. Statistically, women in abusive relationships leave seven times before leaving for good. But he had other plans. He must have sensed that I was leaving because when I came around the corner with bags hanging around my body, one child in tow and the other in my arms, I was greeted with a surprise punch to the face. He snatched our bags from around me and then he placed the kids in the bedroom, while I laid dazed on the floor.

All he kept saying was, "You're never leaving me…ever!" He flipped my dazed body on my face, and he began to straddle me from behind while snatching my pants and panties off. I began to squirm and buck violently until I had rug burns on the side of my face, arms, stomach, and legs. My fighting, flopping, and struggling were futile. He grabbed me by my neck and held me down while he tied me up with a brown extension cord. He began to sodomize me with so much force that I bled for three days after this horrific ordeal.

He did this all while repeating, " You're not going anywhere, and you're going to respect me." And just when I thought it was over, he flipped me over and tried too "passionately" UGH! …make love to me. I threw up in my mouth. I now understand what an out-of-body experience feels like. He then grabbed me by my hair and, ever so, not gently, slammed me onto the couch. He pulled my hair so hard that later, as I was combing it, it filled up the bathroom sink. I was surprised I had any strands of hair left on my head. He kept saying, "Why don't you love me?" Sound familiar?

Now, I am sitting here on the couch, bloody sore and tied up. He then picked up an instrument that was like an ice pick and began tormenting me by poking me and digging this instrument into my skin all over my body. He dug it so deep into my leg that I have a scar to this day. He tortured me, tied up for hours until my body couldn't take anymore, and I passed out. When I came to, I was not just bleeding from my rectum; I was now bleeding from my arms and legs. This episode lasted from the rising of the sun until I saw the beautiful night stars. I looked at the sky and wondered, *How are my babies doing, and when will this nightmare end?*

Open YOUR Eyes

Can you identify any abusive moment(s) that you've suffered?

_____
_____
_____
_____
_____
_____
_____

What are your coping mechanisms as you unpack the abuses you've suffered?

_____
_____
_____
_____
_____
_____
_____
_____
_____

EYE OPENER 4:

Eyes Wide Shut

Time passed, and things were okay. Not great, but okay. But it was like he wasn't used to living in peace. And my God, don't let a special occasion come up and he didn't have any money; that was going to be a fight. Okay, like the time when Mother's Day arrived, and I couldn't even phantom what the fight would be about this time. All I knew was that Mother's Day was to honor me. Welp, before church, he picked a fight. Yep... on this honorable day! Needless to say, I ended up spending Mother's Day lying to everybody at church about how I received this well-rounded shiner on my face. One lie led to other lies, and in my embarrassment to cover the abuse, it gave him the idea that this was an open invitation for more abuse.

The abuse began very subtly, and it gradually got worse. In the beginning, it was only done in private, behind closed doors. Then he didn't care if he was acting an A** in front of his mother and family. I knew it was really bad when he began his tirades in public, in front of strangers.

I remember one time when we went into the store, I had the eldest's hand close to me. Everything was fine until I saw him flirting with a young lady in the store. I snudged him like, 'uh excuse me,' and I said, "Are you freaking kidding me?" The next thing I knew, I started to walk away, and this trick had the nerve to stick out his foot and trip me with a baby in one hand and my daughter next to me. We all went tumbling down. I actually hurt myself, trying to make sure that my babies didn't get hurt. I jumped up so quickly, filled with embarrassment, and said, "What the F**k, you stupid A** B***h, Jesus be a nice mouth on me…. Do you know he had the nerve to say, "I was just playing; your husband can't play with you? Dang!" I looked at him like, is this nut serious? So, I kindly walked out of the store, buckled my babies into their car seats, and sat in the passenger seat until he came out. As you know, he acted as if nothing had happened, and as soon as he was strapped in, I took the car safety belt and started trying to strangle him.

As I was choking and punching him, I turned my body to karate kick him in the head. "N***a, you got me F**ked Up!" My children were in the back, wailing and screaming, "Please stop, Mommy and Daddy. Please STOP!" As I was going for another round to his cranium, I looked at my babies and saw the terror in their eyes and immediately froze. This was not something children should witness. EVER!!!

Another time, was when I confronted him regarding yet another woman. I thank God for protection from any and all STDs. I believe that day, I chose violence again because I was tired of looking stupid and being shamed. It's funny when you think you're hiding a situation, but the outside world sees it as clear as day. We were at his mother's house for a family function, and firstly, I had an attitude on purpose because I didn't want to be there. Secondly, we had unfinished business regarding another woman and had been arguing in the car before arriving. So, anytime he said anything, I felt raunchy and froggy. He asked if he could talk to me in his old bedroom. As I stood up, I began walking with anticipation that there would be a fight. Once he closed the door, he started screaming, "Why are you disrespecting me in front of my family?" I was like, F**k you and F**k your family. I was so freaking angry. He then started choking me, and I just started swinging and kicking. We were hitting every wall in that room. It was so loud! All of a sudden, there was a knock on the door. It was his little sister saying, "Mom said, can you guys keep it down." (Blank Stares, Blink, Blink) Keep it down? Was she seriously going to act like there isn't a brawl at the OK Corral going on in the room right next to hers? At that moment, I knew that if I ever needed help, this was not the place I would find refuge. It was a scary feeling to know that this person could do absolutely anything to me in front of his family, and it would be excused or ignored. If you see something, say something. It may save someone's life.

My Eyes were Wide Shut because I was blinded by the idea of love and the myth of what abuse looked like versus what love and abuse really are. Many women feel that if they're not physically being hit, it's not considered domestic violence. You can be emotionally abused, where your self-esteem is being hit; mentally abused, where your sanity is being hit; even spiritually and financially abused, where your ability to be independent and self-sufficiency is being hit or spiritually abused, where your relationship with God or your religion is being manipulated as a form of control. Therefore, you don't physically have to be hit to be a domestic violence victim. I've encountered some of these red flags below and chose to look over them due to ignorance and the lack of knowledge. Here are some red flags to look for when dating:

- Calls you out of your name or insults you
- Puts you down in private and public
- Gives you the evil stare to try and scare you into submission
- Tries to control who you see
- Threatens to commit suicide
- Threatens to hurt or kill you
- Tries to place wedges between you and your family/friends
- Takes your money or refuses to give you money for expenses such as gas and food

- Prevents you from making your own decisions/always speaking on your behalf
- Tells your children that you are a bad parent or threatens to harm or take away your children
- Prevents you from working or attending school
- Blames you for the abuse
- Gaslighting: acts like you're crazy, you're the problem, or it's your fault that he abused you
- Destroys your property
- Intimidates you with guns, knives, or other weapons
- Shoves, slaps, chokes, or hits you
- Attempts to stop you from pressing charges
- Pressures you to have sex when you don't want to/or in positions that make you uncomfortable
- Prevents you from using birth control
- Pressures you to use drugs or alcohol

Domestic violence doesn't look the same in every relationship because every relationship is different. But the one thing abusive partners have in common is that they will use every trick in the book to gain and keep control.

Because I overlooked the red flags, I'm now living with the ideology of the person I thought I knew, trying to build a family on a rocky foundation. I was hoping that things would get better, only for the monster in my life to show me that things would never be as I dreamed. Of course, with knowledge and coming into the atmosphere of self-love and self-worth, I knew that I couldn't continue to live like this.

Okay, don't judge me.... here I was still living like this, asking myself, why am I still here? I knew I deserved better; however, I was moving forward (mentally) but standing still at the same time (physically). I learned that for some women, they are not ready to leave (there are many factors to consider), and for others, it's not that they don't want to leave, they just don't know how to escape.

Open YOUR Eyes

Have you ever been in a family situation where you saw "red flags"? Did you stand up, ignore them, or make excuses for the exhibiting "red flag" behavior?

_____

_____

_____

_____

_____

_____

Take a moment to examine the reasons why you "did" or "didn't" ignore "red flags."

_____

_____

_____

_____

_____

_____

_____

EYE OPENER 5:

It's Not Just Black and White

Abuse is never just black or white. It has a lot of grey areas. There are many factors equated to each scenario and situation. Never criticize, humiliate, degrade, or belittle a woman who hasn't left her abuser. It takes great courage and strength to pack up and leave, especially when she has children. When she does leave, CONGRATULATE HER!

Here are eight reasons why a woman may stay in an abusive relationship, according to the *Institute for Family Studies* (Whiting, 2016):

1. Distorted Thoughts – Being controlled and hurt is traumatizing, and this leads to confusion, doubt, and even self-blame

2. Damaged Self-Worth – Related to distorted thoughts was the damage to the self that is the result of degrading treatment. Many women felt beaten down and of no value.
3. Fear – The threat of bodily and emotional harm is powerful, and abusers use this to control and keep women trapped.
4. Wanting to be a Savior – Many described a desire to help or love their partners, with the hopes that they could change them.
5. Children – These women also put their children first, sacrificing their own safety to make sure that the abuser's wrath isn't taken out on the kids.
6. Family Expectations and Experiences – Many domestic survivors stated that past experiences with violence distorted their sense of self or of healthy relationships. For example, growing up seeing one or both parents being abused or seeing other family members experiencing abuse.
7. Financial Constraints – Abusers using money as a way to control and manipulate their spouse. Many referred to financial limitations connected to caring for the children or not being able to keep a job because of their abuser's stalking or their injuries causing them to miss work.
8. Isolation – A common tactic of manipulative partners is to separate their victim from family and friends.

Sometimes this is physical, and other times, isolation is emotional.

These are eight common reasons women may stay in an abusive relationship; however, they don't describe every victim and situation. (Remember, that women can also be perpetrators).

Remember, domestic violence doesn't have a color, race, creed, social-economic status, or gender. Women from all walks of life have either experienced or seen some type of abuse in their lifetime. So, when you find out that someone is being abused, be supportive, loving, and understanding - *(see resources located in the back of the book)*.

Open YOUR Eyes

When you read or hear the words "domestic violence," do you feel anything physically? Do you detach? Or do you feel like those words apply to others and not you?

_____
_____
_____
_____
_____
_____

Okay. Dig Deep. What thoughts immediately come to mind regarding "domestic violence"?

_____
_____
_____
_____
_____
_____
_____
_____

EYE OPENER 6:

My Darkest Night

The day that led up to the Darkest Night of my life.......

As always, I came home from work to cook, clean, and take care of the kids. This day was no different, except I was totally over being a wife to a narcissist and sadist human being. It had gotten so bad that I was taking birth control to make sure that I never conceived another child with his DNA mixture. Don't get me wrong, I love my children with all my heart, but it would have been unfair to bring another child into this mess when my heart was grieved that my children had to witness this side of their dad's behavior. I was so serious about him never touching me again, sexually or otherwise. After being diagnosed with ovarian cysts that caused me to bleed 28 days each month for almost a year, I decided to take this show on the road. I went to bed with a pad on every night. Yep, I did this even after the birth control pills prescribed had stopped my bleeding; HALLELUJAH! Anytime I was with him, all he felt was a diaper, TUH!

Okay. Okay, back to my story. I remember getting home and getting ready to cook when I began looking through the mail. I opened the phone bill only to discover that $400 was due. I was like, $400 American dollars? Well, it wasn't me that ran the phone bill this high because, ummmmm.... I was at work! When I brought this to his attention, he went ballistic! Uh, sir, how the hell are you mad that you ran the phone bill up talking to your ex back in Cali, who, from what I found out later, pressed rape charges against you? There were about eight pages with only her number on them. I asked, "Sooooo, how in the hell do you plan on paying the bill because we have kids, and we will need a phone in case of an emergency?" This n***a had the nerve to say, "We'll just have them cut it off." *Blank Stare* IKYFL!!!!! This is when I took my right fist and punched him in his face, and my left hand bashed his skull (It's not okay for women to hit either). Nonetheless, BAE BAE, I was swinging. This allowed him to act mad so that he could go on the date that he had planned earlier. All I'm going to say is, there was a lot of furniture moving before he left. See, I have never been a punk, and I would tear a person's face off; however, a man is stronger than a woman, and my female body got tired after a while. My brain was drained. I was in a marriage with my Eyes Wide Shut, trying to make a relationship work that didn't have the tools to survive. I found my eyes opening as I continued fighting for my self-worth, peace, and happiness.

The biggest fight was with the one that was supposed to be protecting me, my husband, my lover, my enemy.

Jesus…! So only 24 hours had passed since our last WWE match. And in my heart, I knew that my marriage was over. Honestly, it really was over before it started. I kept going over the pros and cons in my head, and the cons kept hitting the ground like a pound of cocaine bricks. I felt that God would be angry with me if I left my marriage. But I had to realize that God doesn't want his children to be sad, mistreated, or abused.

> **SIDENOTE:**
> That's why it's important to have your own relationship with God and not depend on others' opinions to dictate your life.

Ok, I'm back. We had a home, a church, and two kids. Once again, I was the only one working and paying for all of our life choices. So, I went to work, and while at work, I called my sister to do a little rant dump. I couldn't stop talking. She began to tell me that she had a dream. She didn't know what it meant, but she saw me in a life-and-death situation. Mind you; my family didn't know that I was going through physical abuse. Now everybody knew about his infidelity, but not the domestic abuse. All my scars were hidden, and a believable excuse was always available like Google. I was just making stuff up to avoid embarrassment and the judgment and side-eyes that comes along when people find out that a woman hasn't left her abuser after an incident. As we talked, I knew what I needed to do for myself and my children. So, when I got home, I walked in the door saying I WANT A DIVORCE! No, "HI, how was your day?" Just, I WANT A DIVORCE! I was already seven years past due.

I believe I threw him off guard, because in his arrogance, he thought that this would be our lives forever. I know this because he stated a year later that he felt that I never loved him because if I did, I would have taken more than I did. WAIT! WHAT??? Nah, chick a dee. He had seen his mother go through abuse, and she stayed, and in his twisted way of thinking, he equated love with you staying in a relationship no matter how bad you were being treated.

Ummm, nope, I had, had enough, and when I told him that I wanted a divorce, he stated, "Please put that in writing." He placed a paper before me that said that I wouldn't want anything from him when he makes it big in life. And me being De-ne-shia, I took the pen and signed my name so big it took up the whole page. This infuriated him. He ran into the kitchen and took an eight-inch knife. He said, "So you're leaving me?" I said, "YESSSSSSSSS!" And he stood there for a minute looking into my eyes with his eyes turning red and asked me again if I was leaving, and I said, YESSSSSSSSS! This was when he took the knife, and with one quick swipe, he cut my throat. I stood there in disbelief; the blood was warm and sticky as it gushed from my neck. However, his wrath didn't end there. He told me, "If I can't have you, can't nobody have you, and if you don't want me, I would rather die." So, he kept pleading, saying, "Necey, just kill me," and I kept saying,

"No, just go, just leave." It was like a light bulb went off in his head, and he said, "I know how to make you kill me." Now my children at this time were 3 and 5. They shared a room with bunk beds. He stormed into their room and snatched my 3-year-old son off the bottom bunk and out of his sleep. My oldest daughter was sleeping on the top bunk. He had the knife in one hand, my son standing in shock on the other side, and he said, "Now kill me, and if you don't kill me, I'm going to kill him." I was now pleading with the devil to release my son. He was standing there looking like a wild animal. His eyes were as red as crimson, and this was not the first time I had seen him transform from normal to a beast from Revelations right before my eyes. All the while, my neck had not stopped gushing blood. After about an hour of pleading for me and my son's life, I was eventually able to talk him down and out of the house.

I had been using my gown to apply pressure to my neck and after the talk down, I was finally able to go get a towel to stop the pouring of the blood from my neck. I rushed back into the room where my son was standing, with his eyes wide as tea saucers like he had seen a ghost. Unfortunately, my son had seen something no child should ever experience. I remember climbing into his bed, cradling him in my arms, and stroking his head to let him know that Mommy was okay, and I rubbed his head until we both fell asleep.

I also remember calling my dad and telling him that my husband just tried to kill me. I began spilling out everything I had been going through for the past seven years. My dad kept doing this sinister laugh. As I was speaking with my dad, I didn't know that he was loading his gun and packing in preparation to drive from LA to Arizona to kill my abusive husband. Luckily, my bonus mom was able to calm him down and get him out of the car.

Although this was the Darkest Night of my life, it ended up being a catastrophic night for my kids. Our pain didn't end when I left the marriage. It was the beginning of me and my children's journey to facing our traumas and the beginning of our healing process. Both me and my children suffered from PTSD and needed help. According to Kids Health (Cullinan, 2018), "Therapy is a way to get help with a mental health problem or get extra support if you are going through a tough time." A lot of times, therapy is considered taboo, especially in the African American community, and people will shun you and call you crazy if therapy is suggested.

I grew up in a time when we were told as children that, "What goes on in this house, stays in this house." I understand not to be blabbing, "I saw mommy and her friend doing the Bamba bounce stretch in her room." BUT, if you're being hurt, SAY SOMETHING! I don't care who is the one hurting you; SAY SOMETHING! If you are going through or have gone through trauma or even witnessed trauma, please talk with someone. Help is available. (Check resources in the back of the book)

Mental illness is real. Sometimes mental illness is not something that you're born with. It can also be caused by

LIFE! According to *Office on Women's Health* (OASH) (2018), "Abuse can have so many effects on your body, such as obesity, arthritis, mood and personality disorders, heart disease, and post-traumatic stress disorder (PTSD)."

I suffer from PTSD and occasionally have mini episodes to this day. According to my doctor's diagnosis, due to severe trauma and the stresses that my body endured, I had two miscarriages, almost lost sight in my left eye due to many punches to the face, and my heart muscles are permanently weak. We only have one body, one life, and saying something when you're being hurt is a form of self-care.

Open YOUR Eyes

Have you ever been to therapy? Why or why not? Does the thought of going to therapy make you relieved? Or does the thought of therapy make you uncomfortable?

_____
_____
_____
_____
_____
_____
_____

Is there a person that is a family, friend, or confidant, that makes speaking your feelings a soft place to land?

_____
_____
_____
_____
_____
_____
_____

EYE OPENER 7:

The Comeback

I didn't press charges, which was a big mistake that I regret to this day. I just wanted him gone and out of my life. I feel like I could have saved other women from going through what I did if I had only pressed charges, and for that, I'M SORRY. When my ex was forced to go back to Cali from Arizona, he had the audacity to tell me again that he felt that I never loved him because if I really loved him, I would have taken more than what I did. What the HELL! I told him that if that's what helps you sleep at night, have at it, just get the F**k out of here. Can you believe that there are people in these streets with this type of thinking? Okay, I'm back. So, when he left, he took the car, the dog, and all the money out of our checking account. Remember, I was the only one working and had just gotten paid. So now I was left with absolutely nothing; no money, no food, no phone, and no transportation to get to work. At this time, remember my children were 3 and 5 years old, looking at me to make something happen. It was rough. I didn't know where and how to get the resources we needed to survive because we were in unknown territory.

Here I was in Arizona, looking at bus schedules to go and apply for food services and trying to connect with co-workers to get a ride to work every day. The day that I made my appointment to get help from the government assistance program, it was cold, and my children were hungry. I was able to make the money that my mother sent me to stretch like a rubber band. Once we got there, the office was cold and dirty, and the seats were broken, but I needed help! Honestly, I was just another number there, but I needed what they provided. Blessed be to God, I had an excellent caseworker that began giving me information and resources needed to rebuild my life.

One day, my mom called and said, "Necey, I have an extra car you can use. Just come down and get it." It was a big black-bodied Mercedes; we called her Big Bertha. She was a blessing. She had leather interior, new tires, and no AC. I got her in the winter, but BAE BAE, by the summer, when Arizona reached 118 degrees on average, Big Bertha was trying to strangle us in that Hot Box. But we had trans-por-tation. (Insert me dropping it like it's hot).

I found us all therapists because our lives had been turned topsy turvy. It wasn't business as usual; I was left to pick up the pieces for all of our lives as the narcissist went to prey on others. After the darkest night of our lives, doing everyday things like dropping off my kids at school was hard. My daughter kept a lot of her feelings inside and was quiet. On the other hand, my son would lash out and begin mimicking seen abusive behavior. He would also blurt out to anyone that would listen, "My dad tried to kill my mom." For weeks, I would drop him off at school, he would scream, claw, and fight the teachers because he didn't want me to leave. He would say, "You're not coming back because the MONSTER is going to kill you." At 3 going on 4, his mind equated his dad's behavior to that of a monster. One day, he was with a group of kids in a dance class, and according to the teacher, the room was quiet, and he just blurted out, "MY DAD TRIED TO KILL MY MOM."

When she called me to tell me what happened, I was so embarrassed because I hadn't fully taken the time to deal with my own pain and humiliation. And here is my son saying in his own way, I'M NOT OK! Remember, trauma doesn't just affect one person. It affects the entire household. Get help. Please don't suffer in silence because of shame, embarrassment, or humiliation. (Check out the resources in the back of the book).

Side Note: When you take steps to heal from abuse, you have to unlearn the behaviors that were learned to survive in order to survive the behaviors that were learned. Also, make sure that you're not making decisions in your present state based on the trauma experiences of the past.

My comeback game was strong. We had begun to rebuild our lives. I recall an evening that I was on my new cell phone (insert my Snoop Dogg's dance) with my baby sister, watching TV in the living room, and the kids were also in the living room playing. My daughter was laughing and being goofy when all of a sudden, my son let out this hearty laugh from his belly, and the room fell silent. This is significant because my son stopped laughing after the age of 18 months. My sister asked, "Was that my nephew laughing?" And I said, "YESSSSSSS!" Our hearts were overwhelmed with joy and our eyes were filled with tears. My life at that moment was starting to make sense. We had started living.

After another year in Arizona, we moved back to Cali on January 1, 2000. The moment I set foot on Cali soil, I tried to file for a divorce, but the courts stated that I had to be a California resident for six months before filing. No problem. I set my calendar for July 1, 2000. Because who was not playing was me. During this time, I opened and operated a daycare, which I ran for ten years. I went back to school and graduated in 2004 with my AS degree in Early Childhood Development. Oh, and I celebrated my divorce that was granted on February 17, 2004. My ex-husband gave me such a hard time with the divorce. He wouldn't show up to court, he would physically try to fight me when we needed to get papers notarized, or he simply wouldn't sign the papers. I would have to start certain parts of the process over because some of the paperwork was time-sensitive. Despite him trying to prolong the inevitable, the judge stated that she would be granting my divorce immediately because I had been fighting for almost four years to get my divorce. I didn't have to wait the usual six months. My God, me and my baby sister toasted, laughed, and cried because I was free. We all were still undergoing therapy; however, we were LIVING IN FREEDOM.

I taught as a preschool teacher for seven years, where I met and loved so many kids. I have one that stole my heart and to this day is my baby. But I felt I should be doing more, so I went back to school, and I graduated Magna Cum Laude in 2017 with a BS in Human Development for Women and Children. I wanted to understand the different facets of trauma through different colored lenses. Domestic Violence looks different and is handled differently in each culture. Some cultures will disown the woman if she leaves her abusive partners. While other cultures tell women that if the man is taking care of the home, do what you can to make it work. I learned that the deaf community tends to stay in an abusive situation because they don't feel welcomed or understood in the hearing community. Once again, trauma and abuse are not just Black or White. There's a whole lot of GREY.

During this journey called life, I realized that everything happens for a reason. I didn't understand it at first. But, after my divorce, I was so angry, bitter, and defensive. I lived in a bubble where I was never going to allow myself to be treated like trash again. Don't get me wrong, I am still a work in progress. I had to unlearn survival tactics and take the flight or freeze response from my memory bank. With God, my family/friends, and a life coach, I am healing from the inside out. It hasn't been easy or a quick transition, but with every step, you take forward, is progress that needs and will be CELEBRATED!

Through my experiences, my nonprofit House of Loving Hands was birthed. HOLH is a nonprofit that assists abused women and their children with emergency shelter (i.e., hotel stays), food, clothing, and resources. We seek to empower, encourage, and support women and their children. We proudly service families that live in the Richmond Contra Costa Area/Bay Area. We teach a multitude of skills to empower women to self-sufficiency and facilitate the reacclimating of our participants back to society.

Our mission is to establish a safe haven for abused women and their children. We work diligently to get our participants back on their feet through counseling, therapy, group sessions, job training, love, and support. We work to build the self-esteem of the women we serve by celebrating their accomplishments so they can stand on their own platform of success. Our prayer is that the families we serve are healed from the inside out.

Domestic violence impacts all races, religions, economic levels, education levels and genders. My lived experiences and education have led me to understand the fundamentals of abuse and how to navigate through the healing process. Here at House of Loving Hands, our motto is: You're Not

Alone, It's Not Okay, and It's Not Your Fault. I AM MY SISTER'S KEEPER!

Thank you!

Open YOUR Eyes

What would you say if you could summarize your story in 3 sentences?

_____
_____
_____
_____
_____
_____

Who would be the first person you would want to share your story with?

_____
_____
_____
_____
_____
_____
_____
_____

EPILOGUE:

Wrapping It Up

Remember, this story is through the lenses of my eyes and life experiences. And because my children also dealt with trauma through my trauma, they also have slowed, still pictures captured through their lenses. A lot of times, when we are dealing with women who have suffered abuse, we set up services and support for them to navigate through the pain. However, we can't forget that the children were unwilling participants in the drama and trauma and have to get the support, help, and therapy needed to thrive. Children who live in homes plagued by physical abuse, molestation, incest, and parents with addictions suffer PTSD. If you have been or are being abused, please say something. That cliché, "What goes on in this house, stays in this house," is OUT THE DOOR. Speak up. Someone will listen and get you the help needed. (Resources are located in the back).

HOUSE OF LOVING HANDS IS HERE FOR YOU!

REFERENCES

Cullinan, C.C. (2018, March). *Taking Your Child to A Therapist.* Kids Health.
https://kidshealth.org/en/parents/finding-therapist.html

Medline Plus, National Library (2021, January 19). *What is DNA?*
https://medlineplus.gov/genetics/understanding/basics/dna/

Office on Women's Health (2018, August 28). *Abuse, Trauma, and Mental Health.* OASH.
https://www.womenshealth.gov/mental-health/abuse-trauma-and-mental-health

Whiting, J. (2016, July 21). *Eight reasons women stay in Abusive Relationships.* Institute for Family Studies.
https://ifstudies.org/blog/eight-reasons-women-stay-in-abusive-relationships

RESOURCES

National Hotline Numbers/Contra Costa County Numbers

Domestic Violence Resources	Mental Health Resources	Homeless Resources
House of Loving Hands Crisis Hotline 510-730-1162	Contra Costa County Mental Health Services Crisis 24 Hotline 925-646-2800	Homeless Hotline 1-800-808-6444
National Suicide Prevention Hotline 988	Richmond Crisis 510-374-3061	National Child Abuse Hotline 1-800-422-4453
National Domestic Violence Hotline 1-800-799-7233	John Muir Behavioral Health Center 925-674-4100 1-800-680-6555	Community Violence Solutions 1-800-670-7273
Contra Costa Crisis Center Homeless Hotline 1-800-808-6444	Rubicon Programs Inc., 510-235-1516	A Step Forward 1-925-685-9670 EX101
Bay Area Rescue Mission 510-215-4860	Reach Project 925-754-3673	Center for Child Protection at Children's Hospital 510-428-3742
GRIP 510-233-2141	West County Adult Mental Health Services 510-215-3730	
A Safe Place 510-986-8600	Access Line 1-800-491-9099	
Shelter Inc 925-335-0698	Detox Facility 1-866-866-7496	
Hotline 211	Access Alameda 510-567-8100	

My Destiny Transitional 510-654-4420 Saffron Strand 510-778-9492 510-275-9494 Appian House 1-800-610-9400 Brookside Shelter 1-800-799-6599 Contra Costa Interfaith Housing 925-944-2244 FESCO The Family Shelter 510-581-3223 Heather House 707-427-8566 Nierika House 925-676-9768 Shelter Intake Line for CCC 1-800-799-6599 Winter Nights Program (October-May) 925-933-6030		

AUTHOR'S BIO

Deneshia Clemons was born and raised in San Francisco, California. She is the proud mother of 4 beautiful children and the owner/founder of House of Loving Hands. Before she started her journey of becoming an author, Deneshia received an AS in Early Childhood Development from Contra Costa College. After that,  she taught for seven years at St. David School as a preschool teacher. She then continued her education at Cal State East Bay with great courage, and graduated Magna Cum Laude with a BA in Human Development for Women.

Deneshia is now an advocate for women and their children, that have suffered at the hands of abuse. She works, and has made her home in Richmond, CA, with her loving family, friends, and nonprofit.